Tribal Coloring Book

Designed By
Megan L. Fox

ISBN:1530109078
ISBN-13:9781530109074

Color Test Page

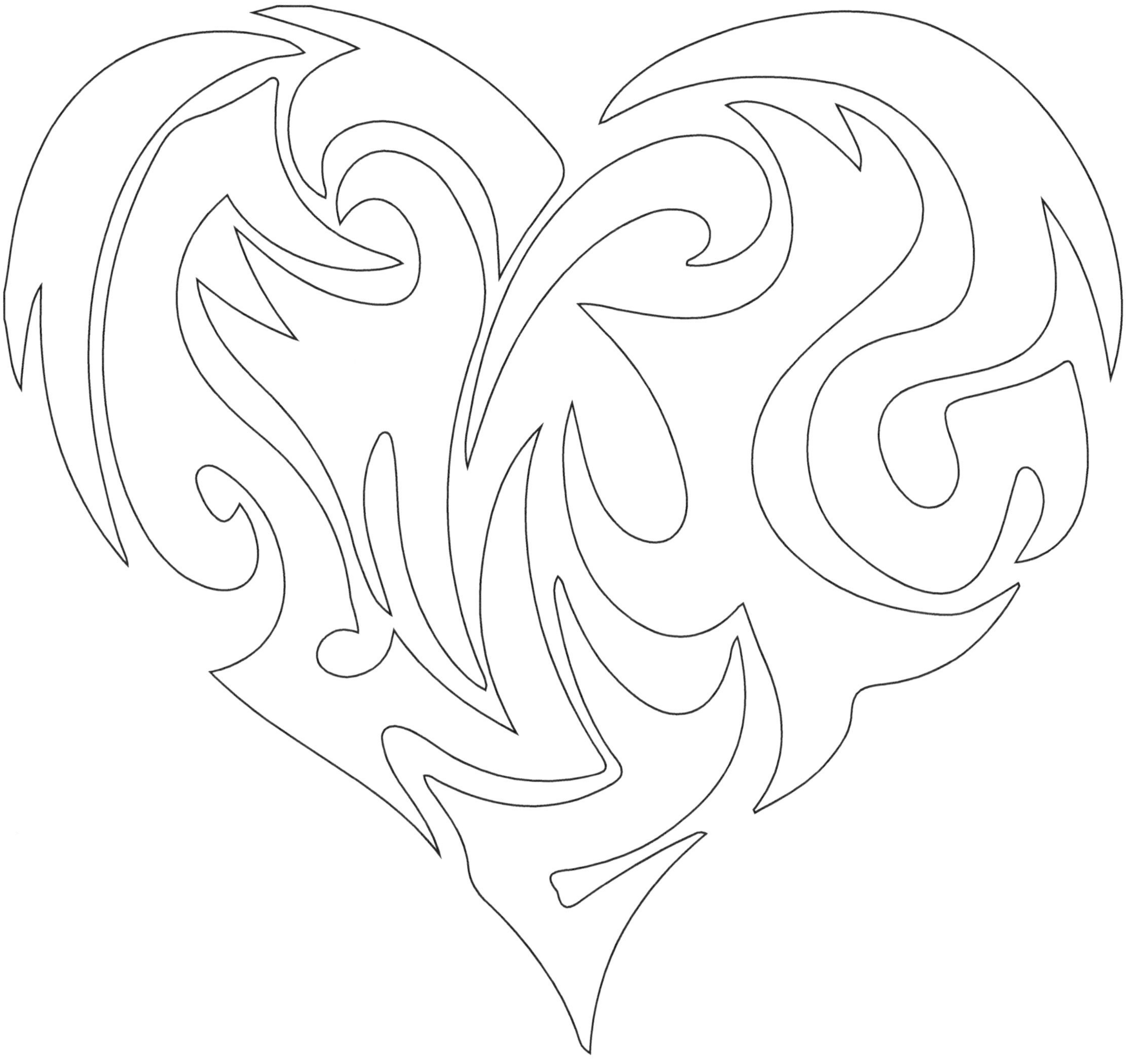

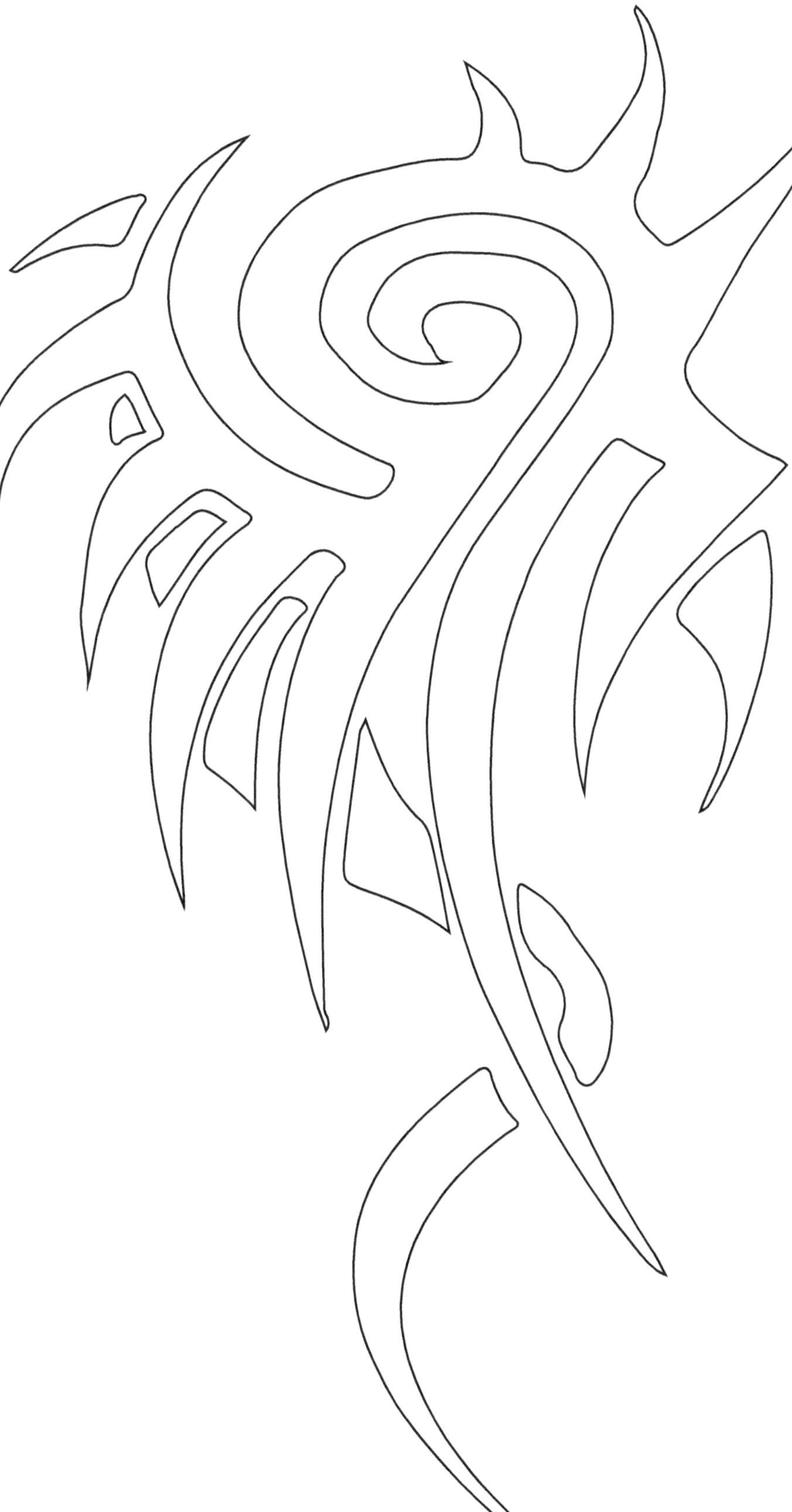

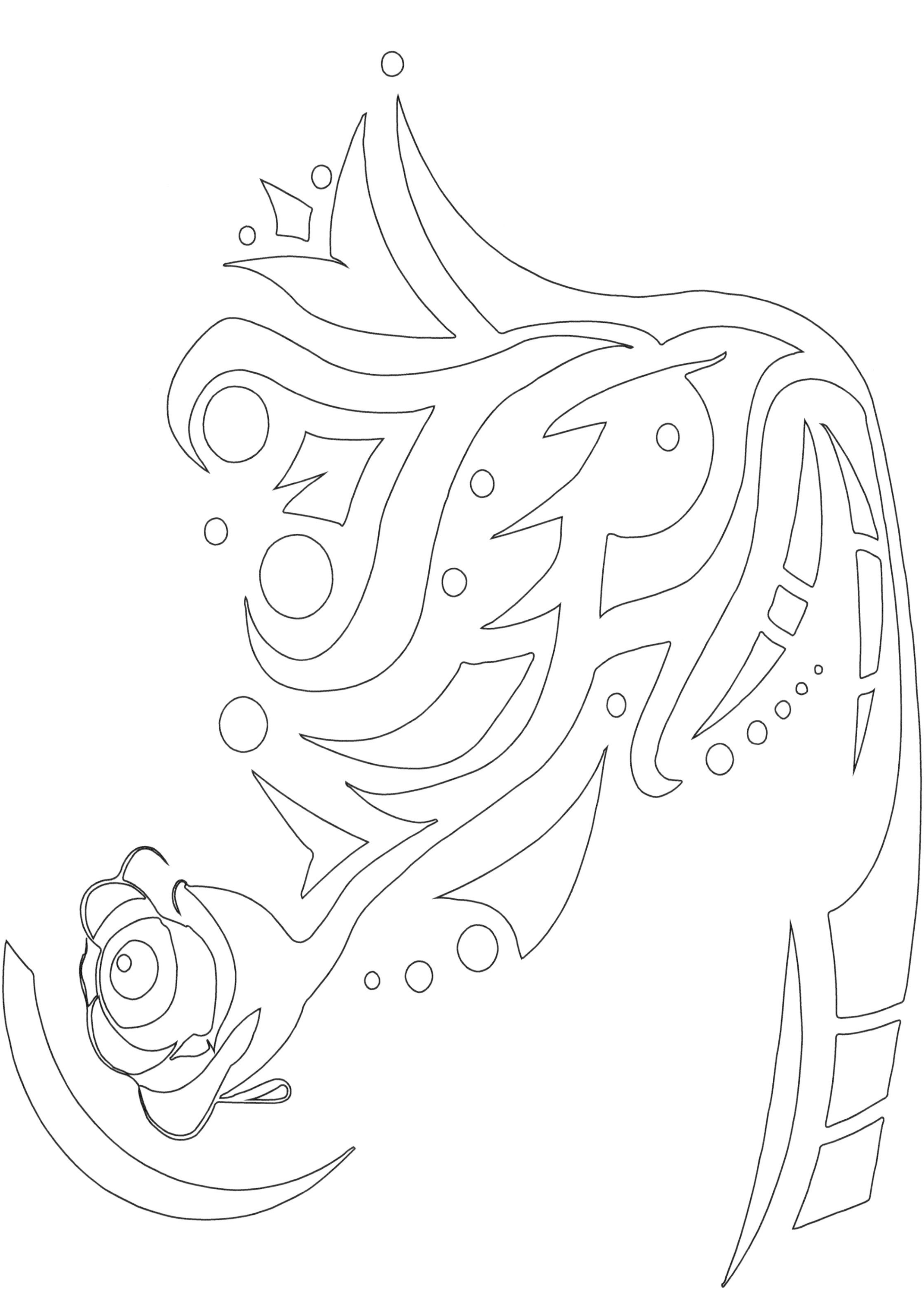

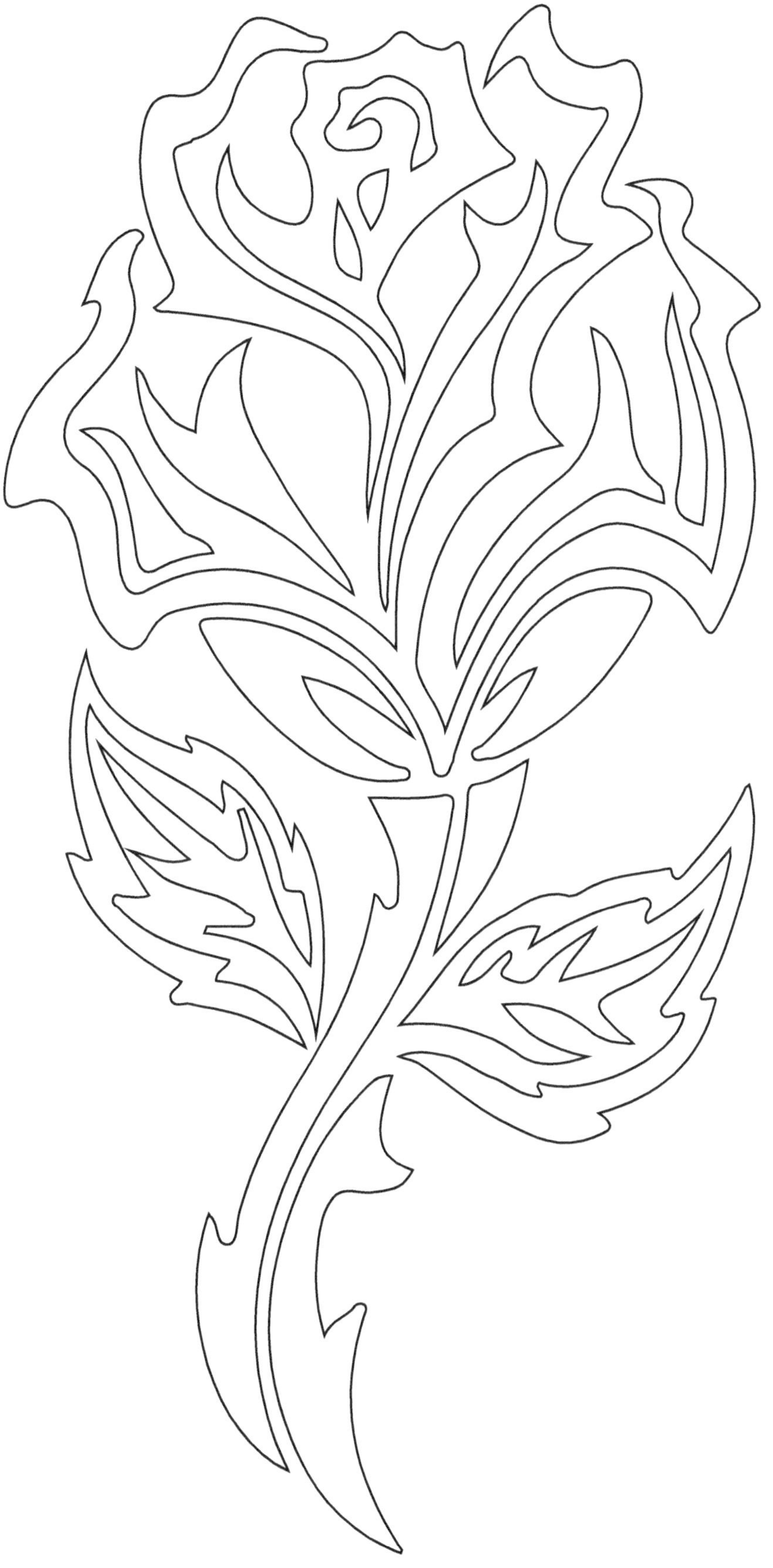

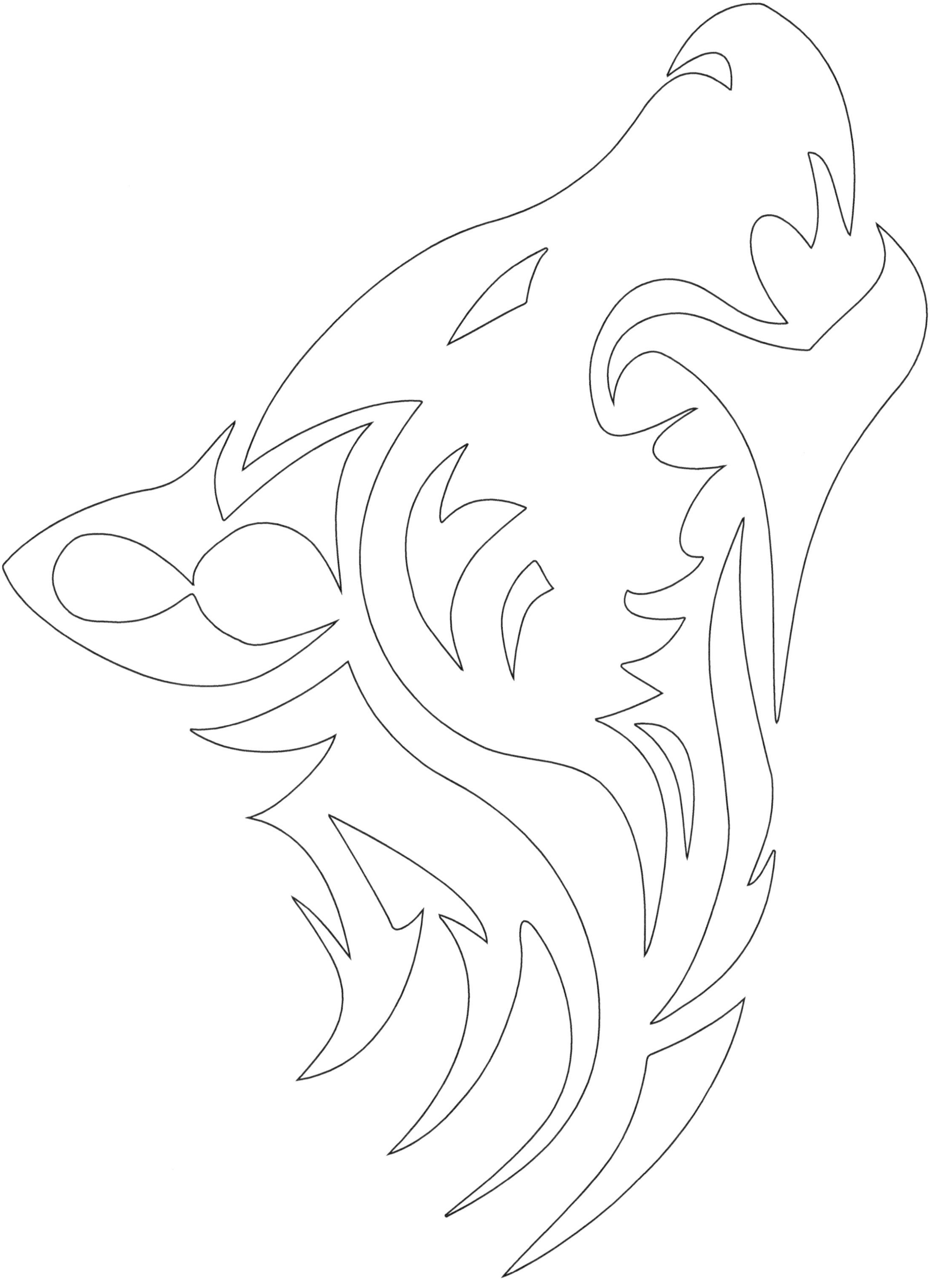

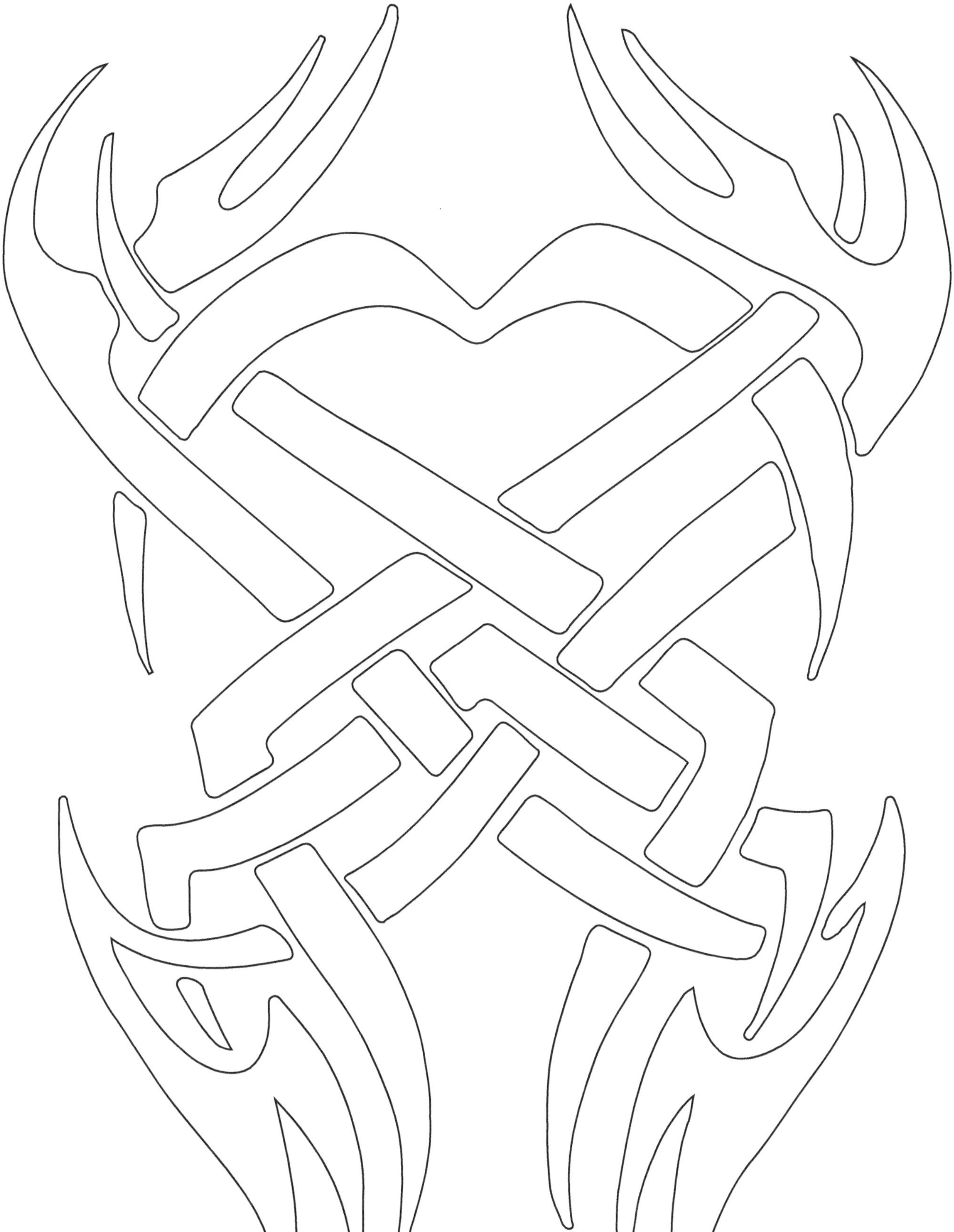

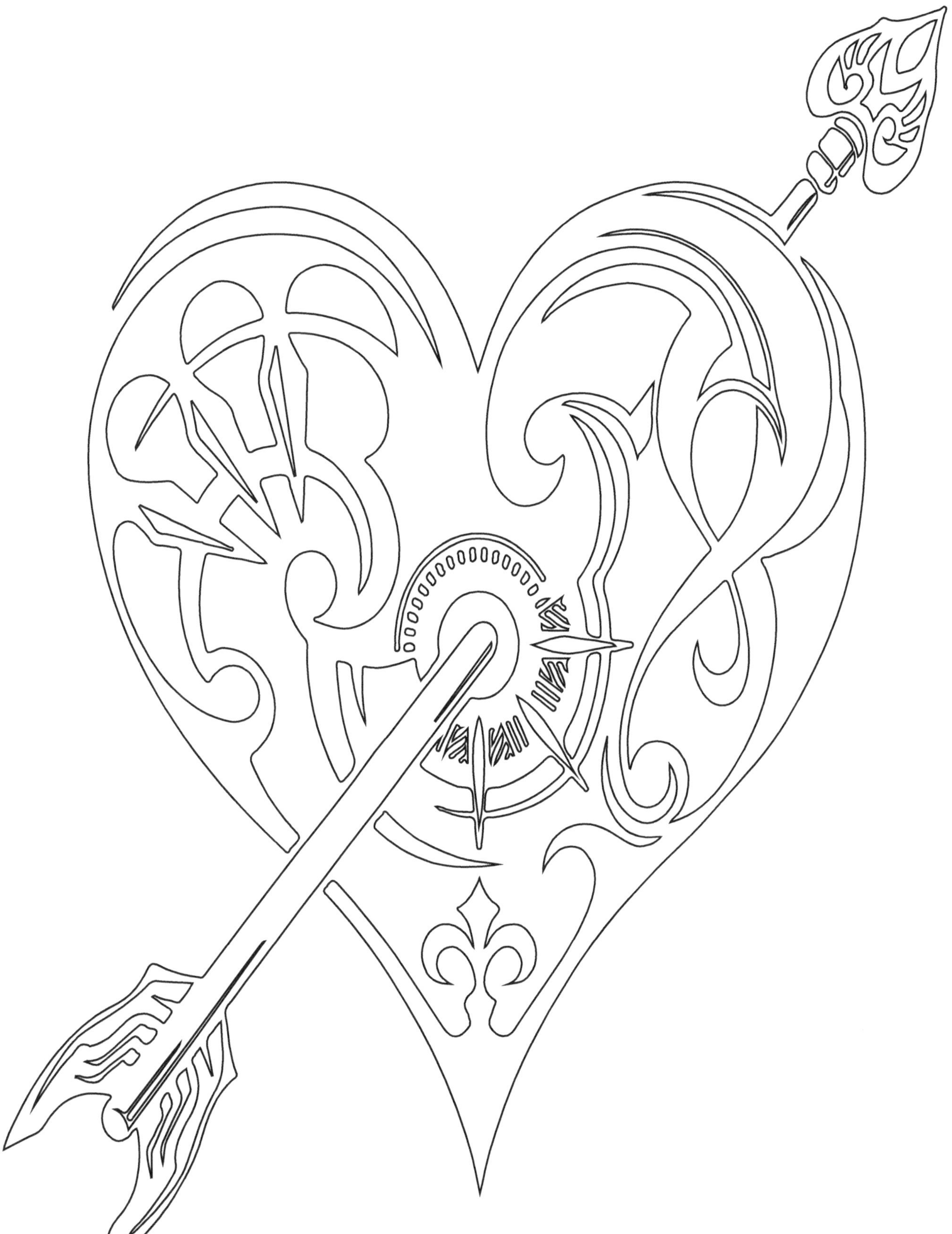

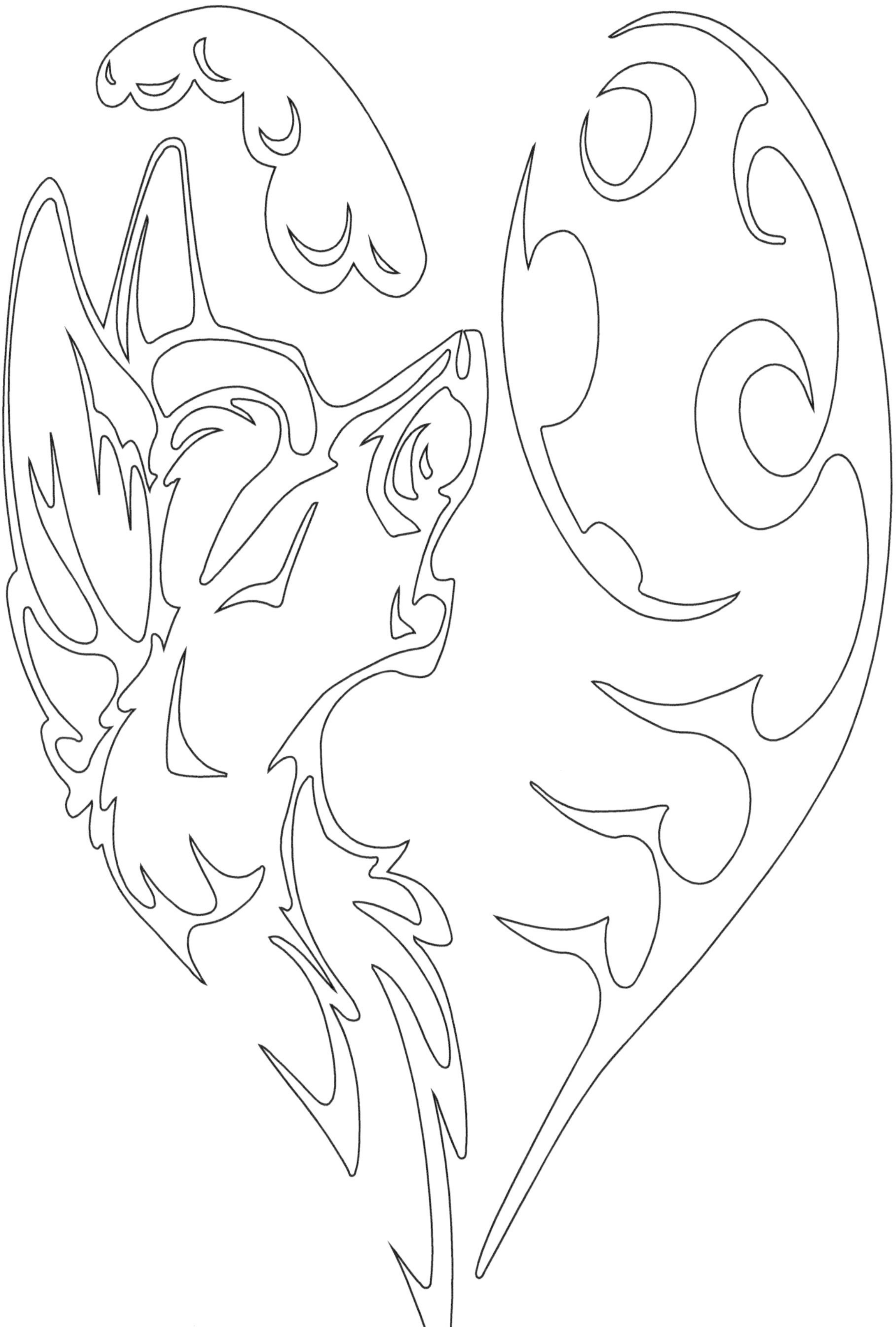

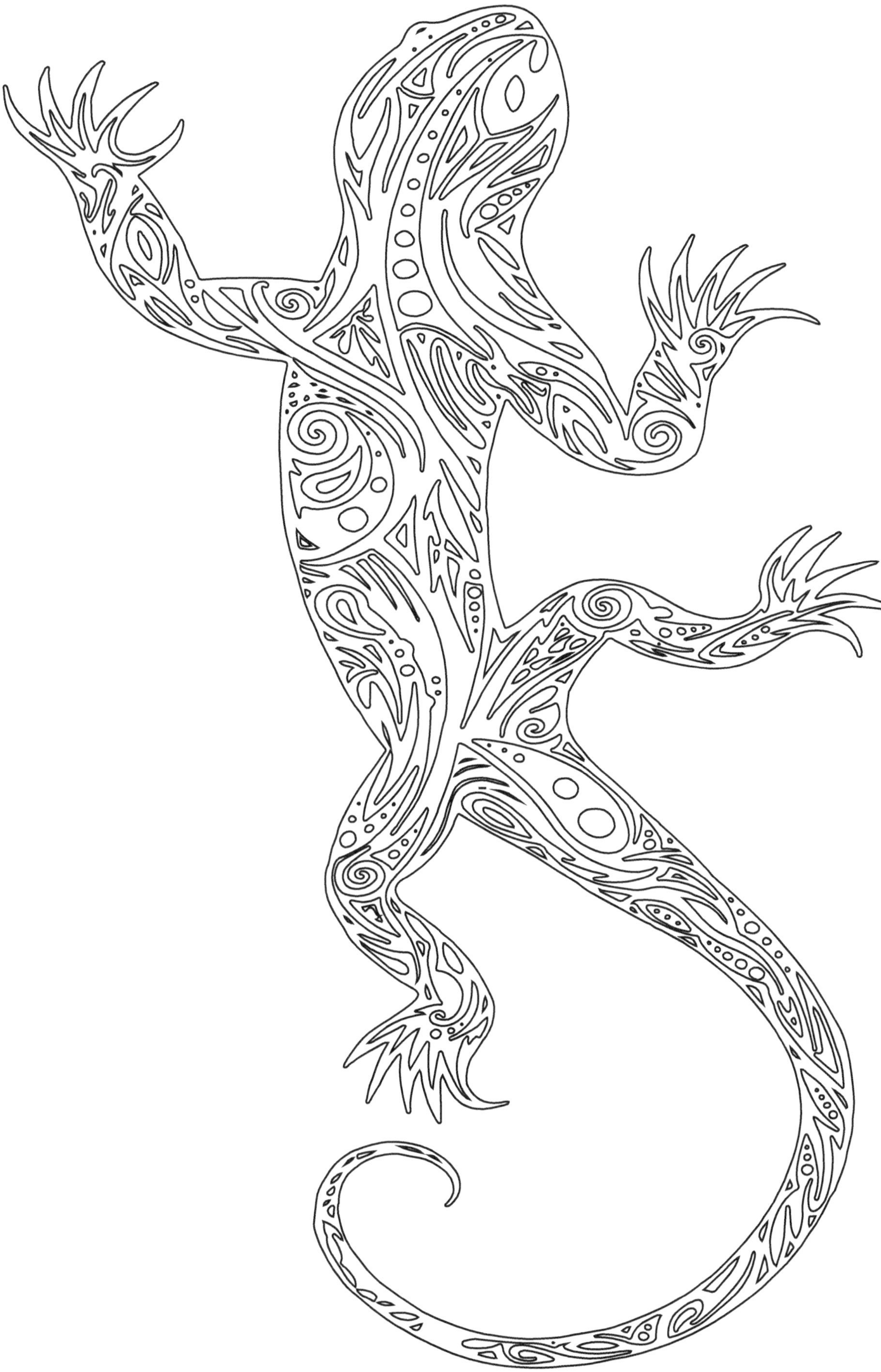

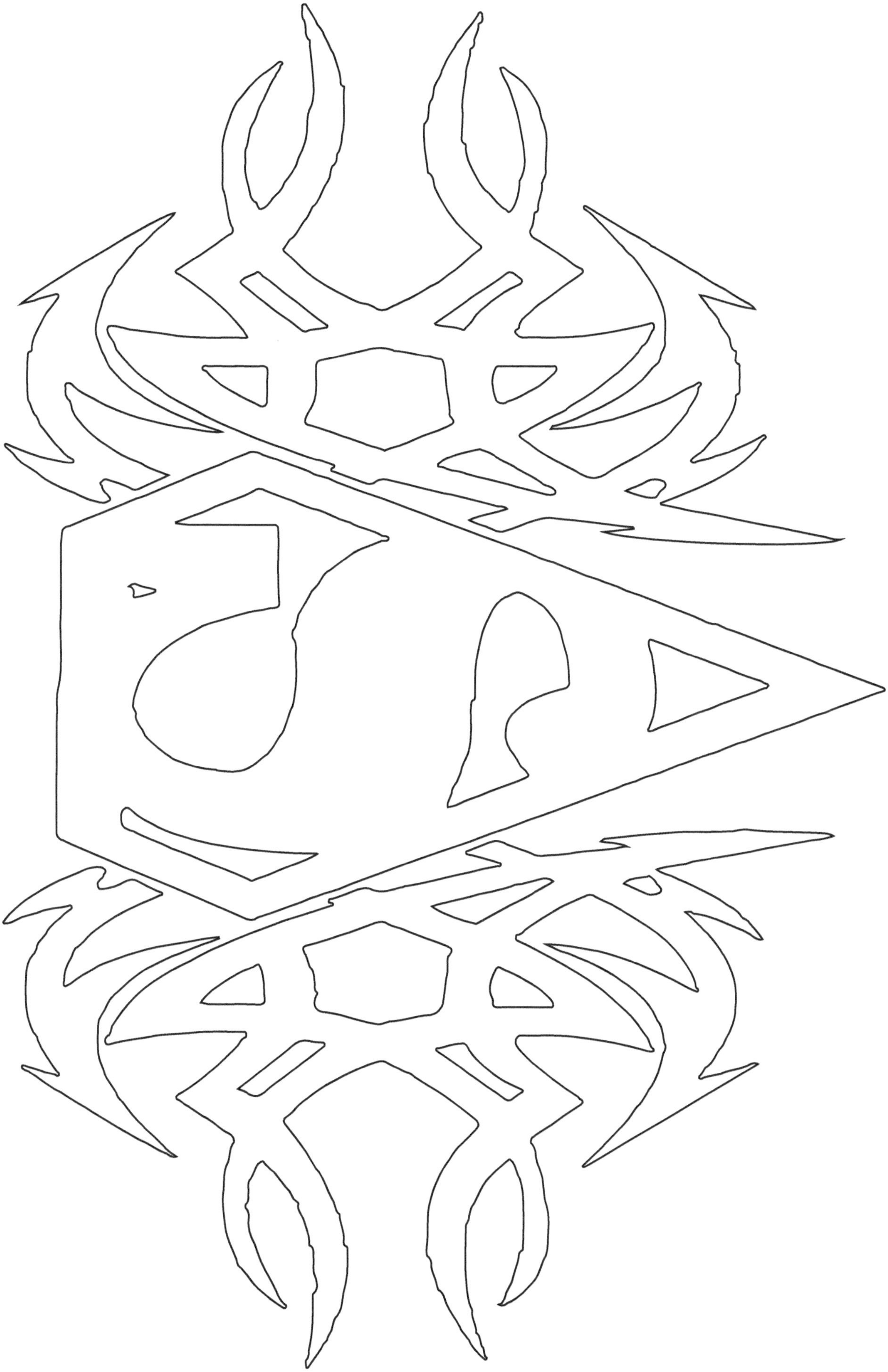

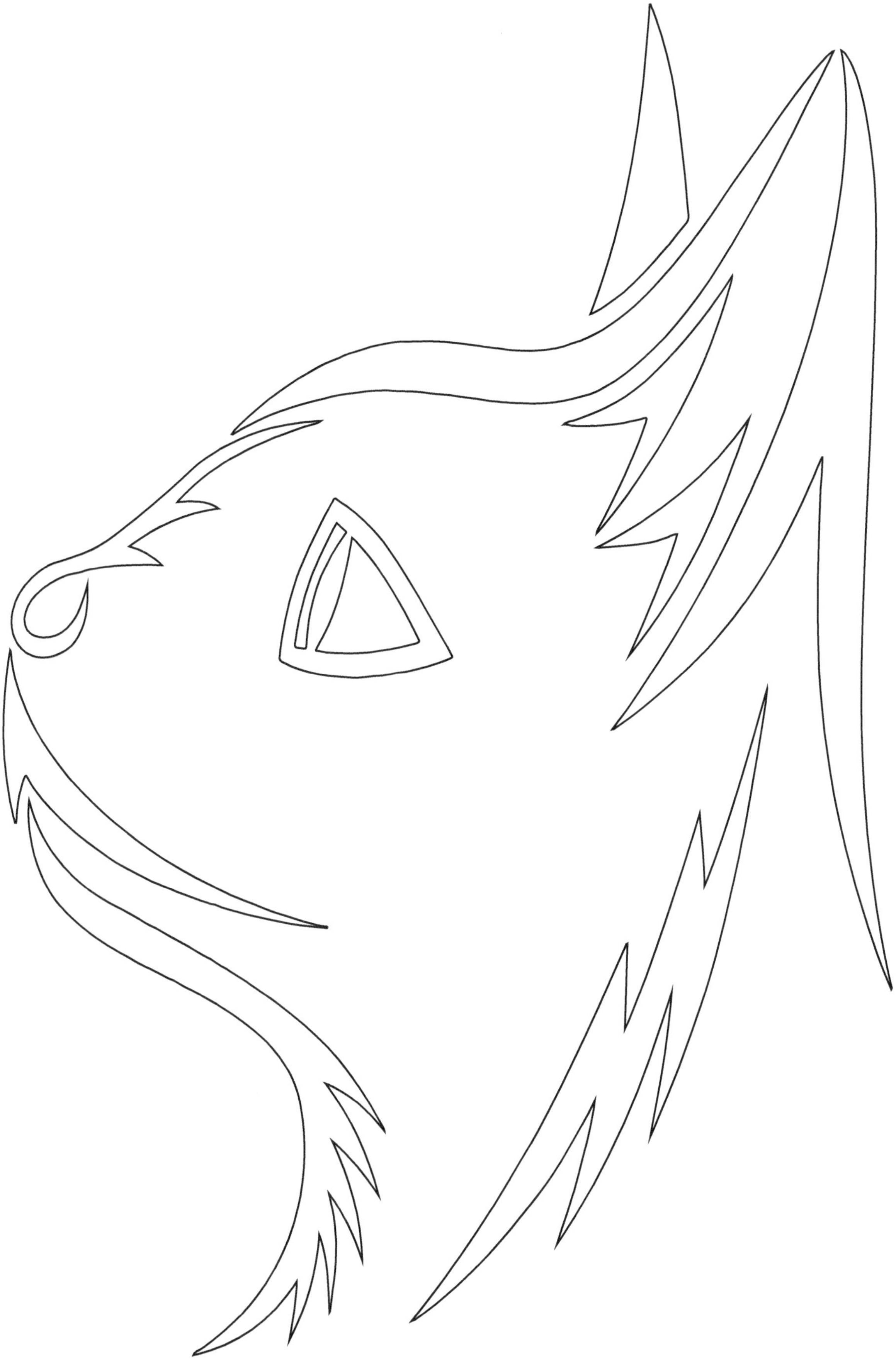

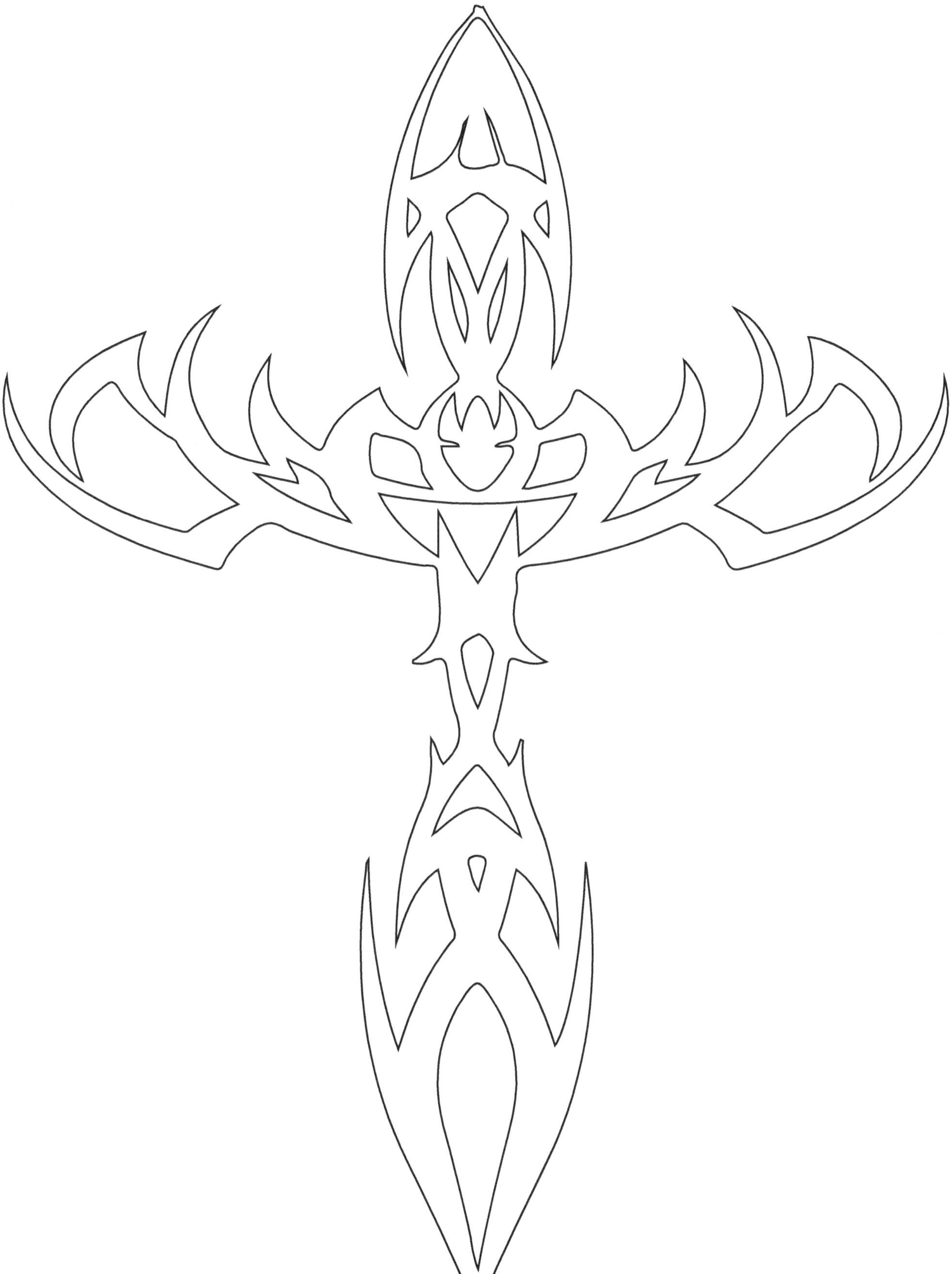

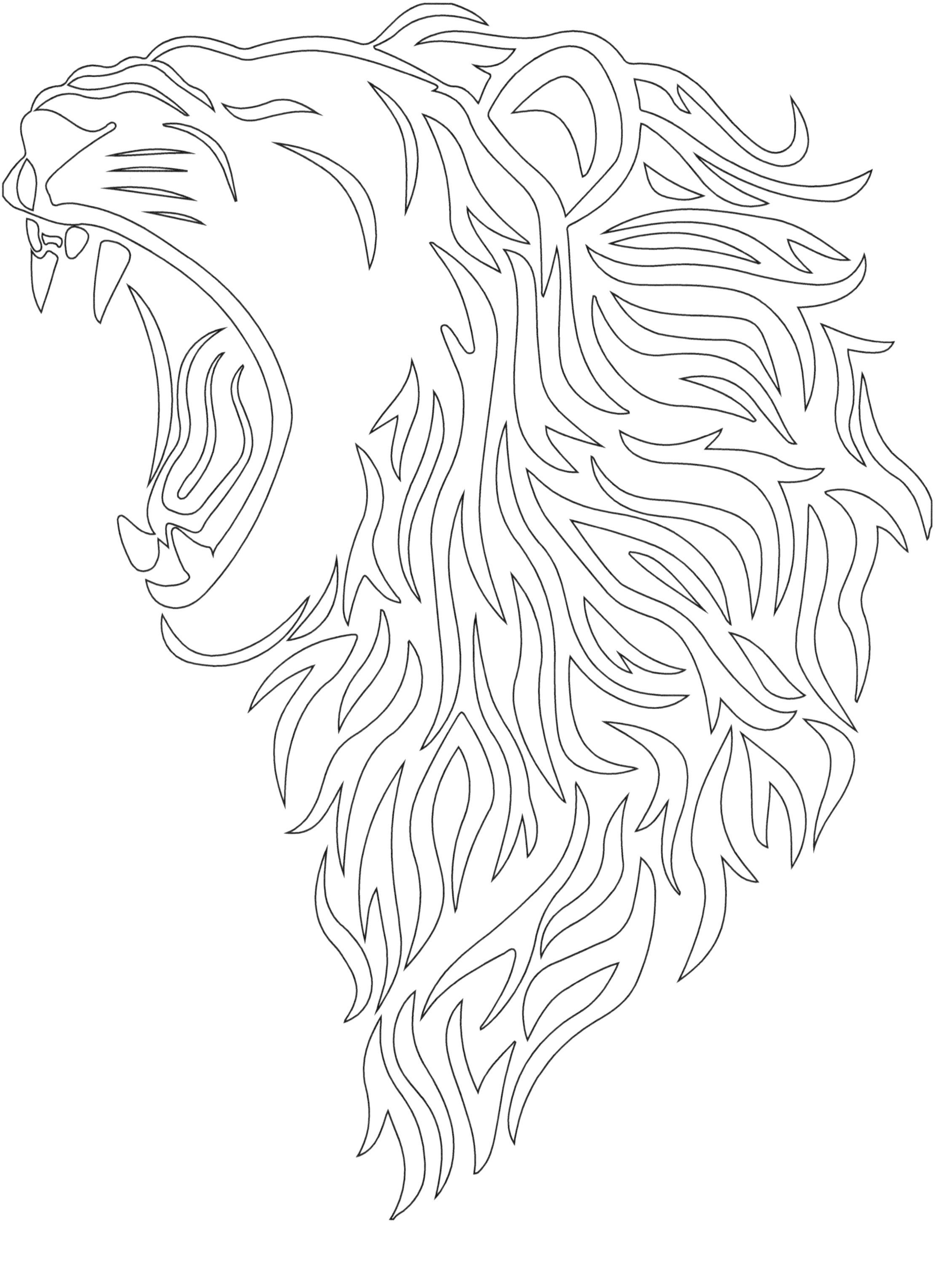

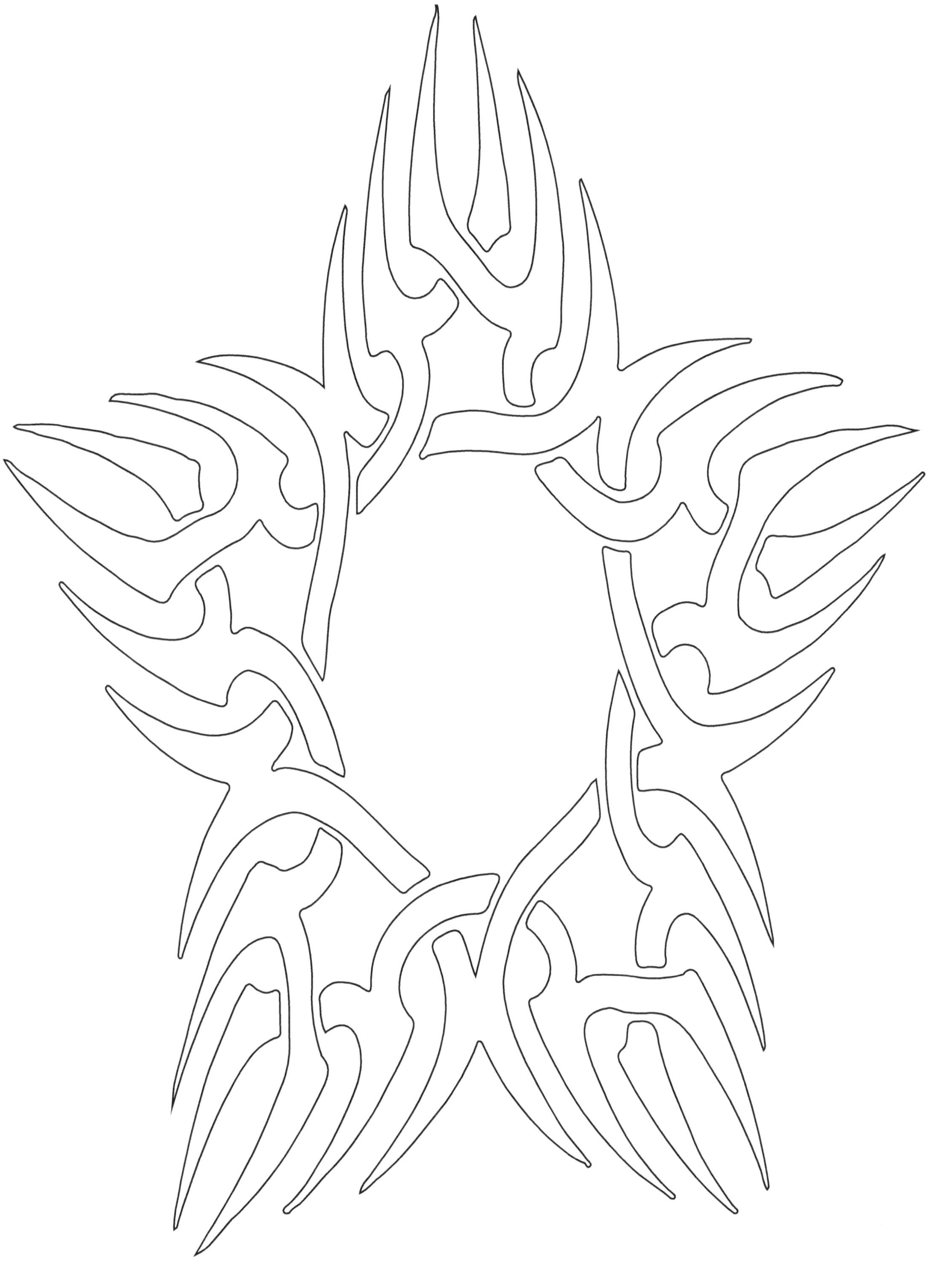

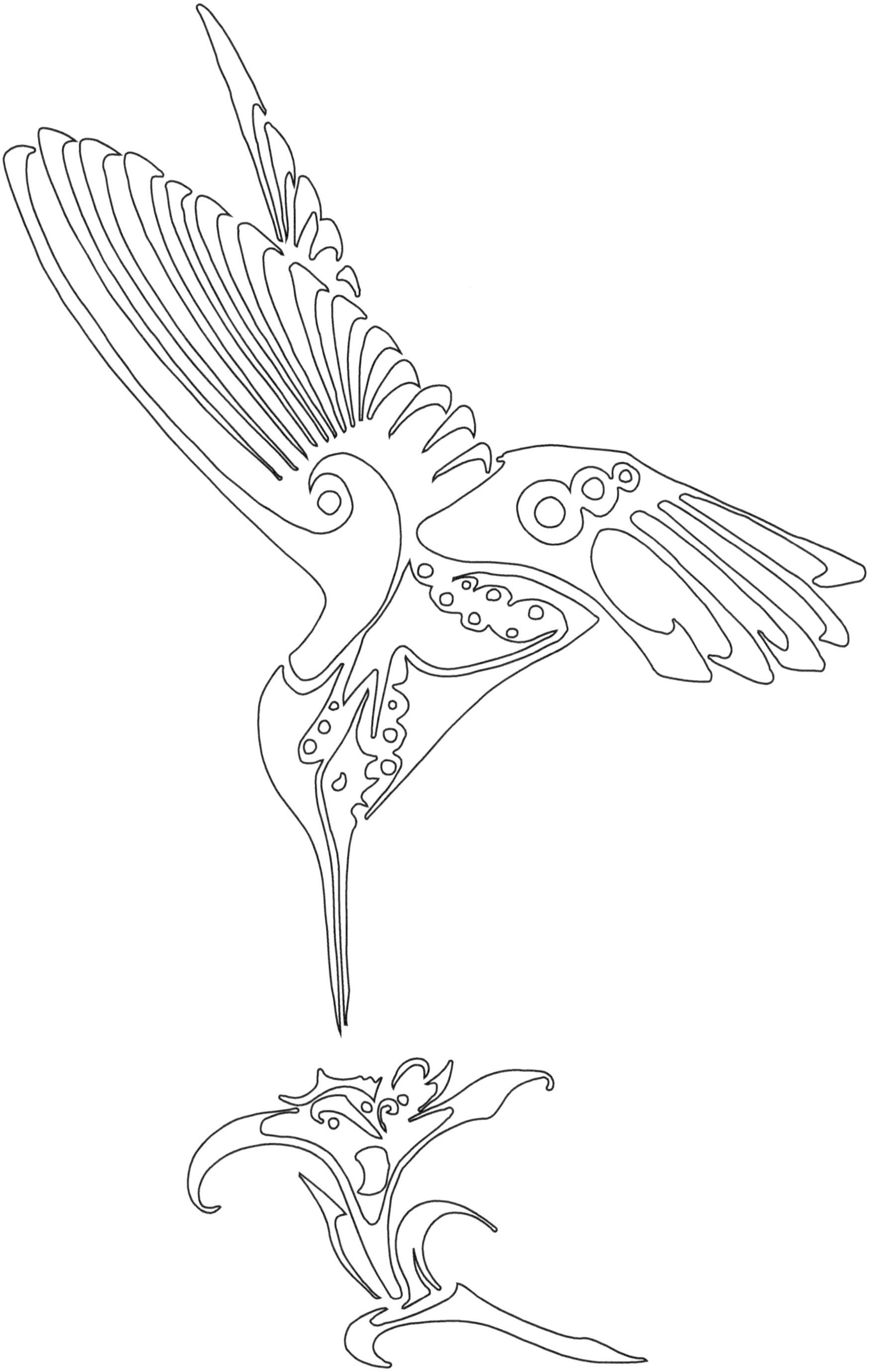

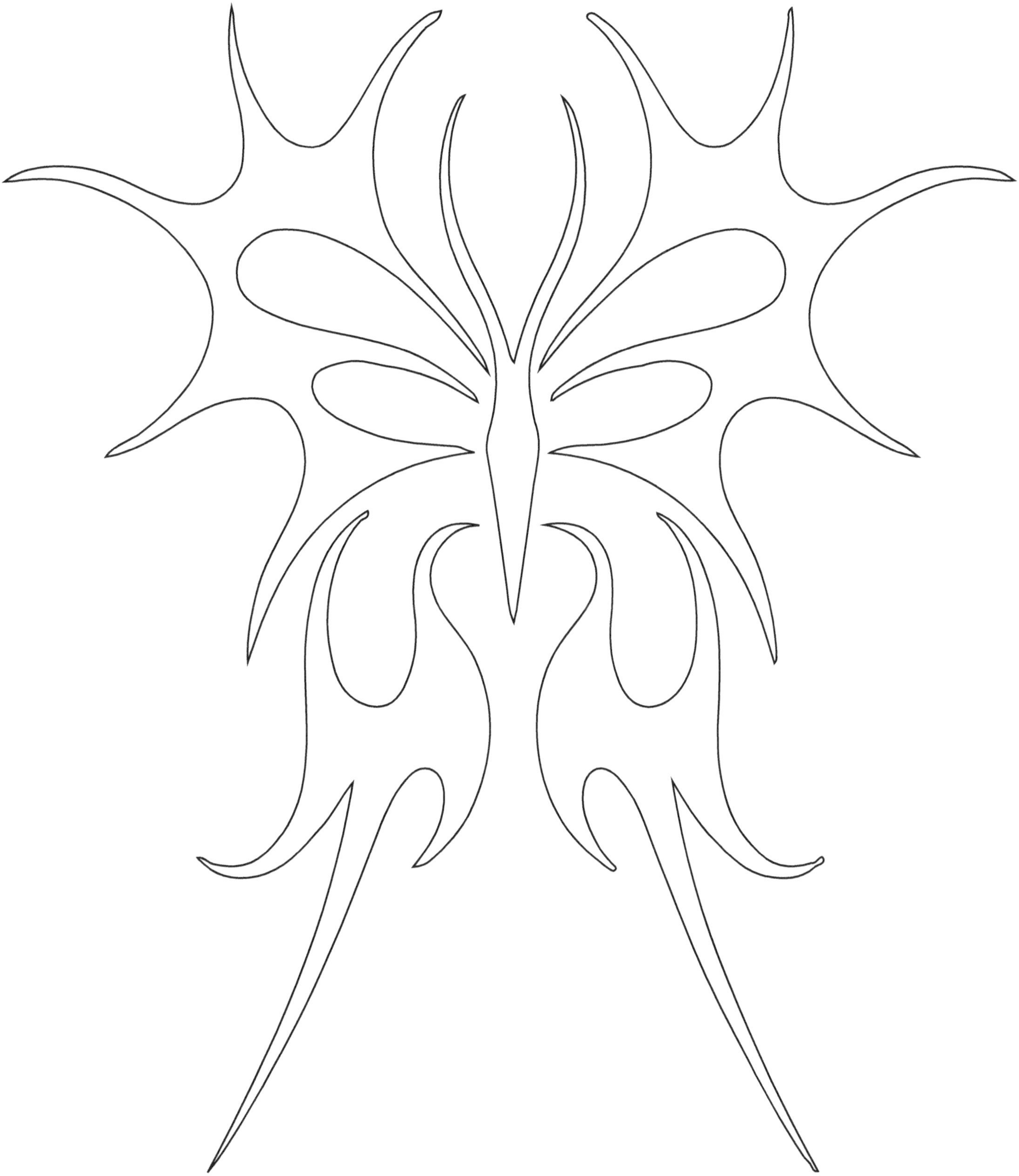

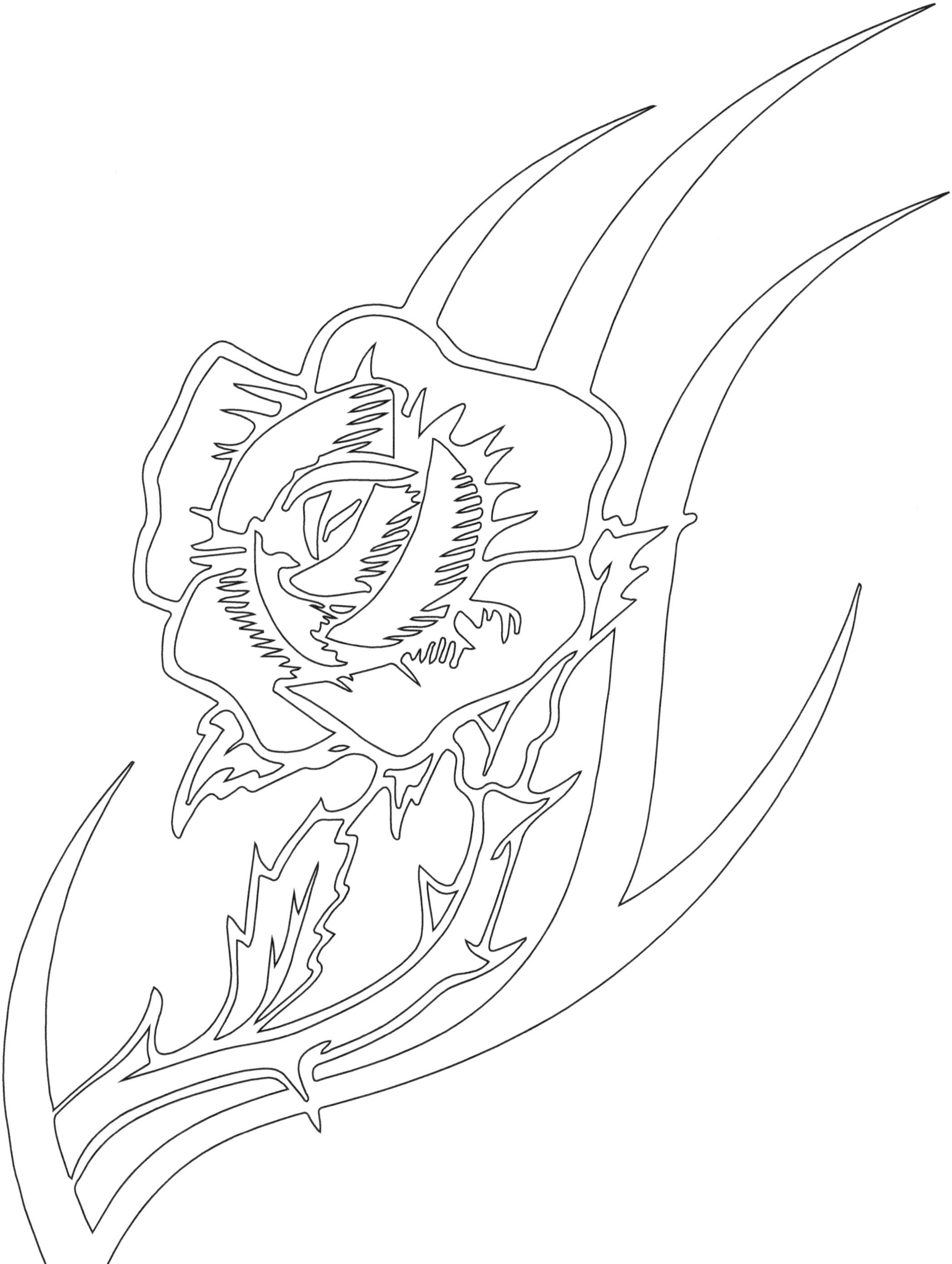

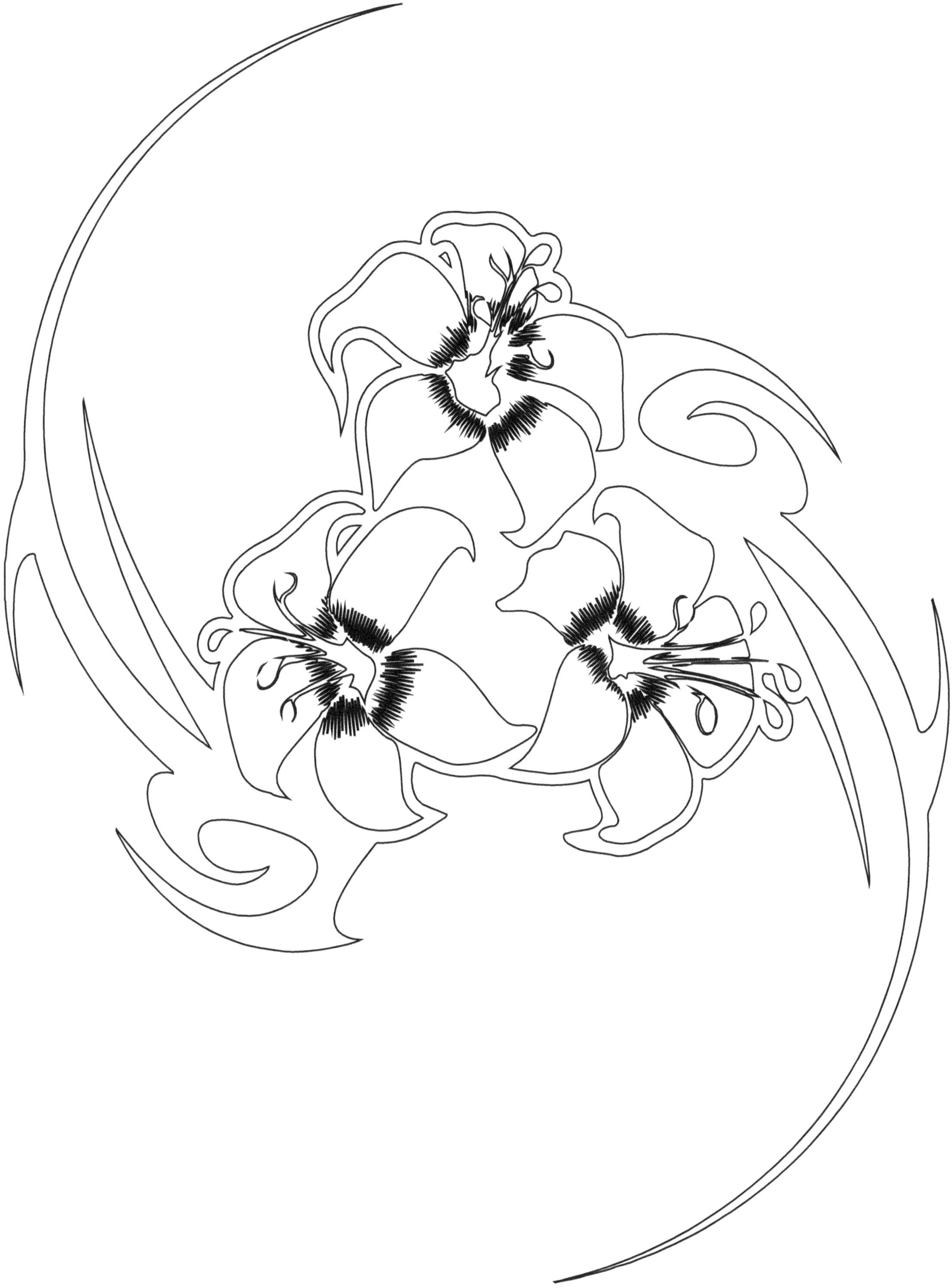

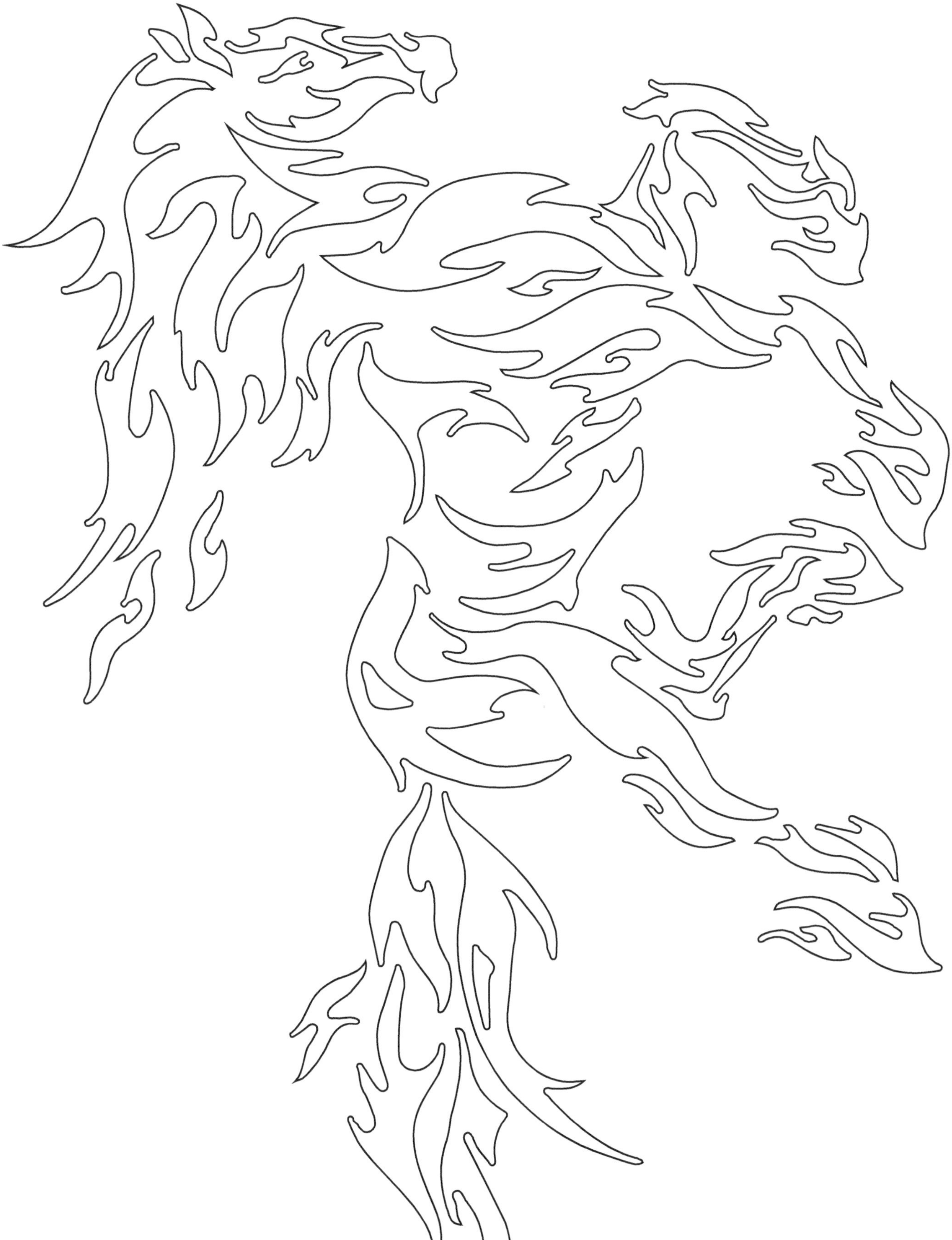

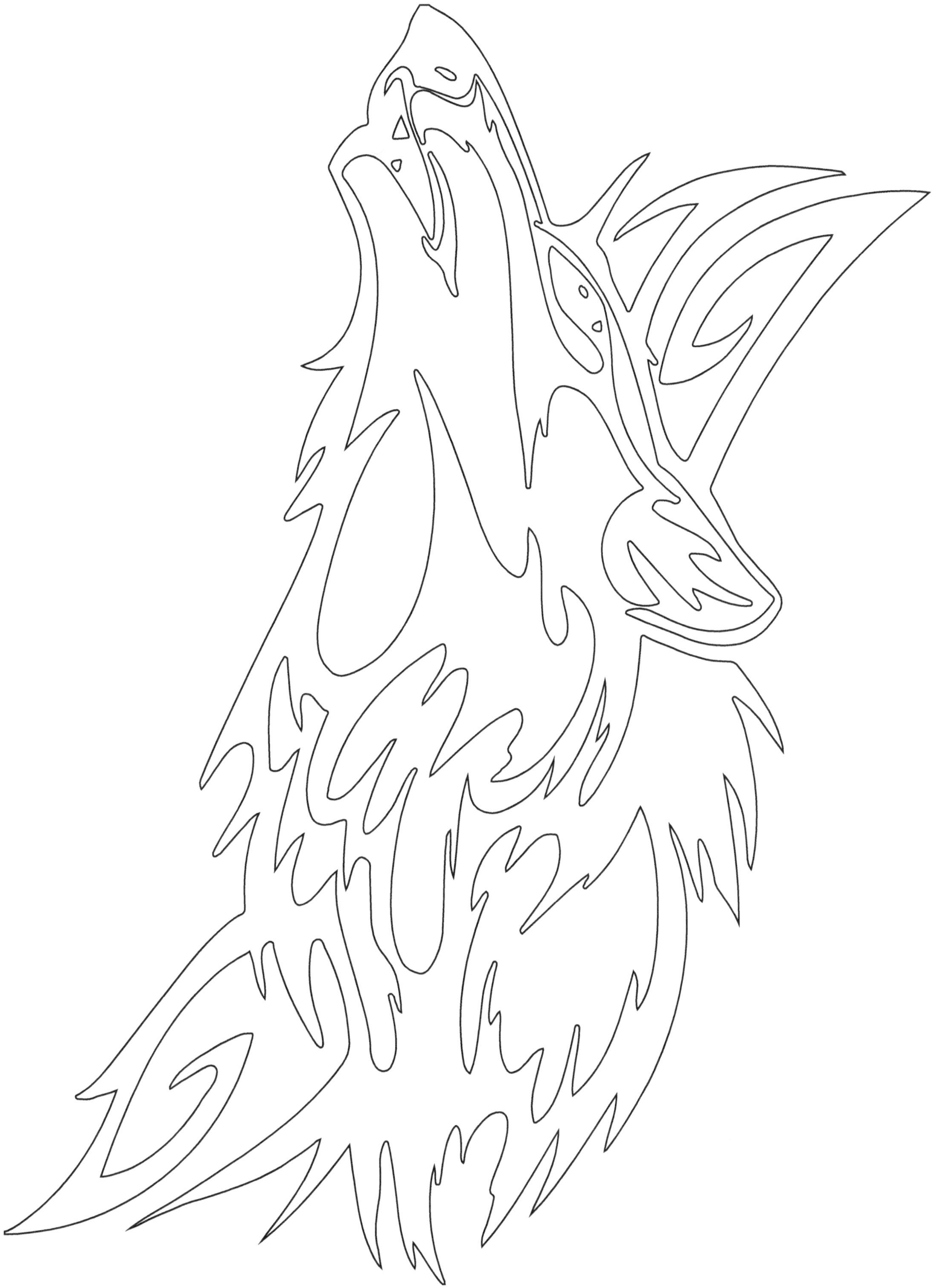

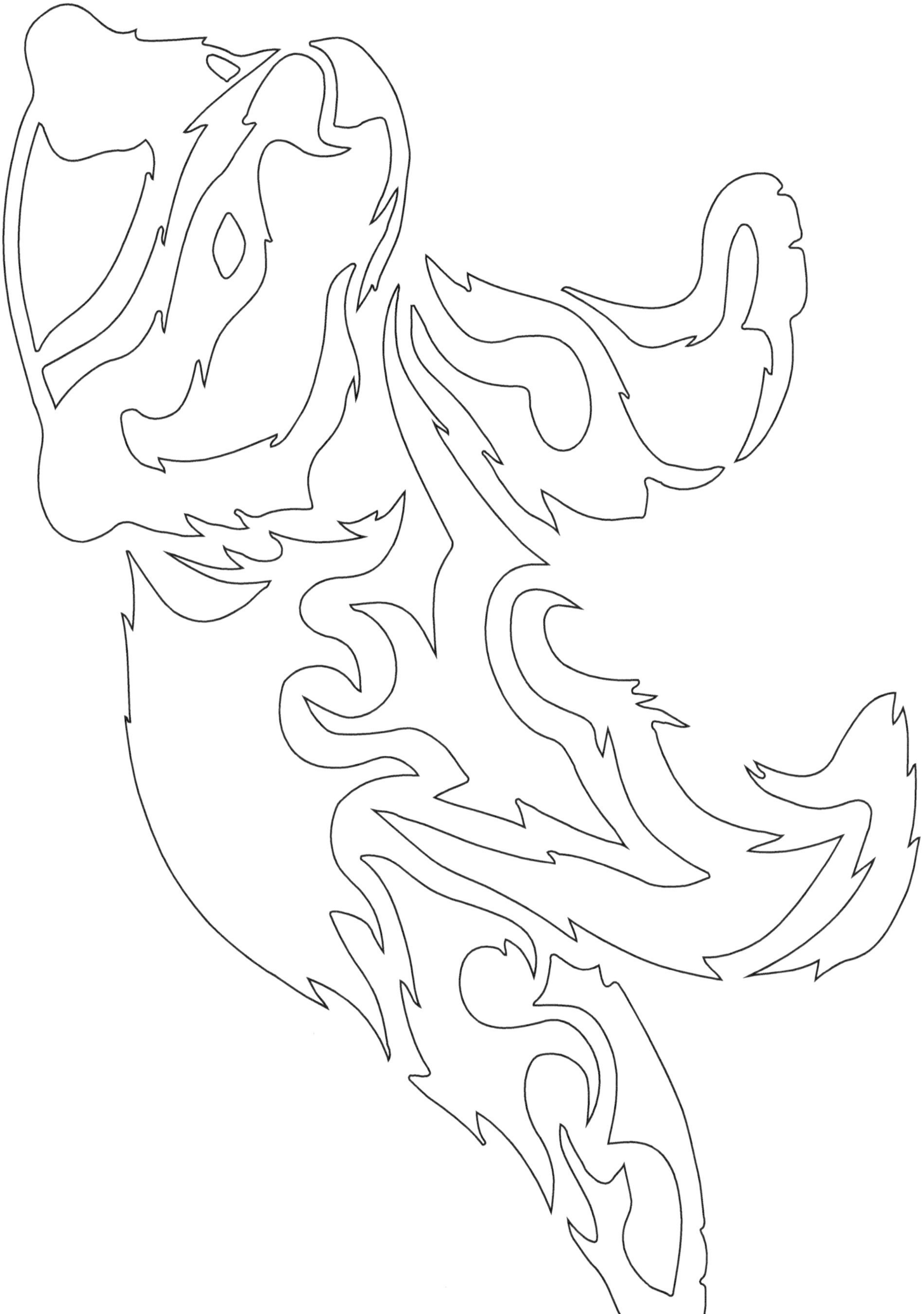

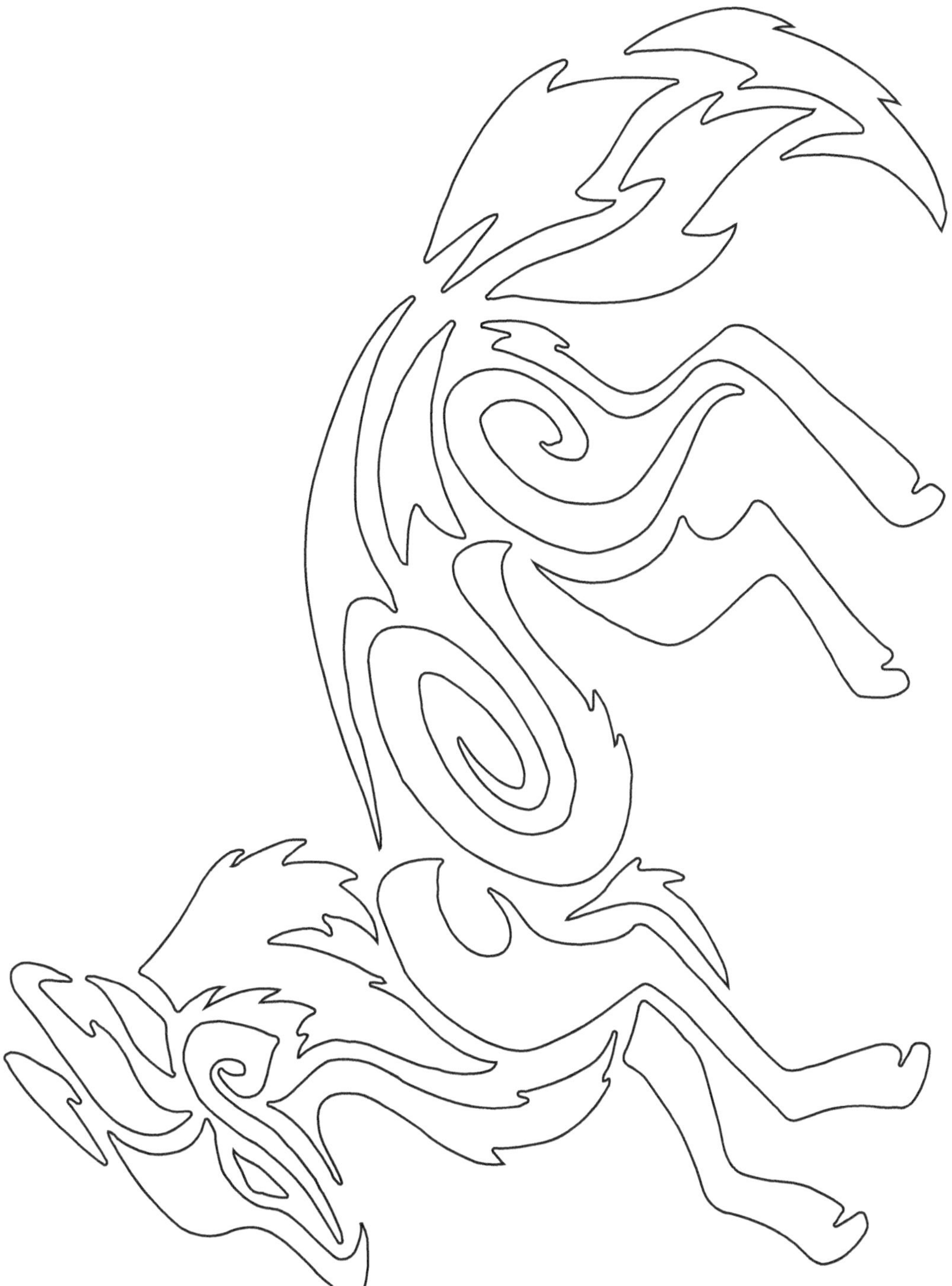

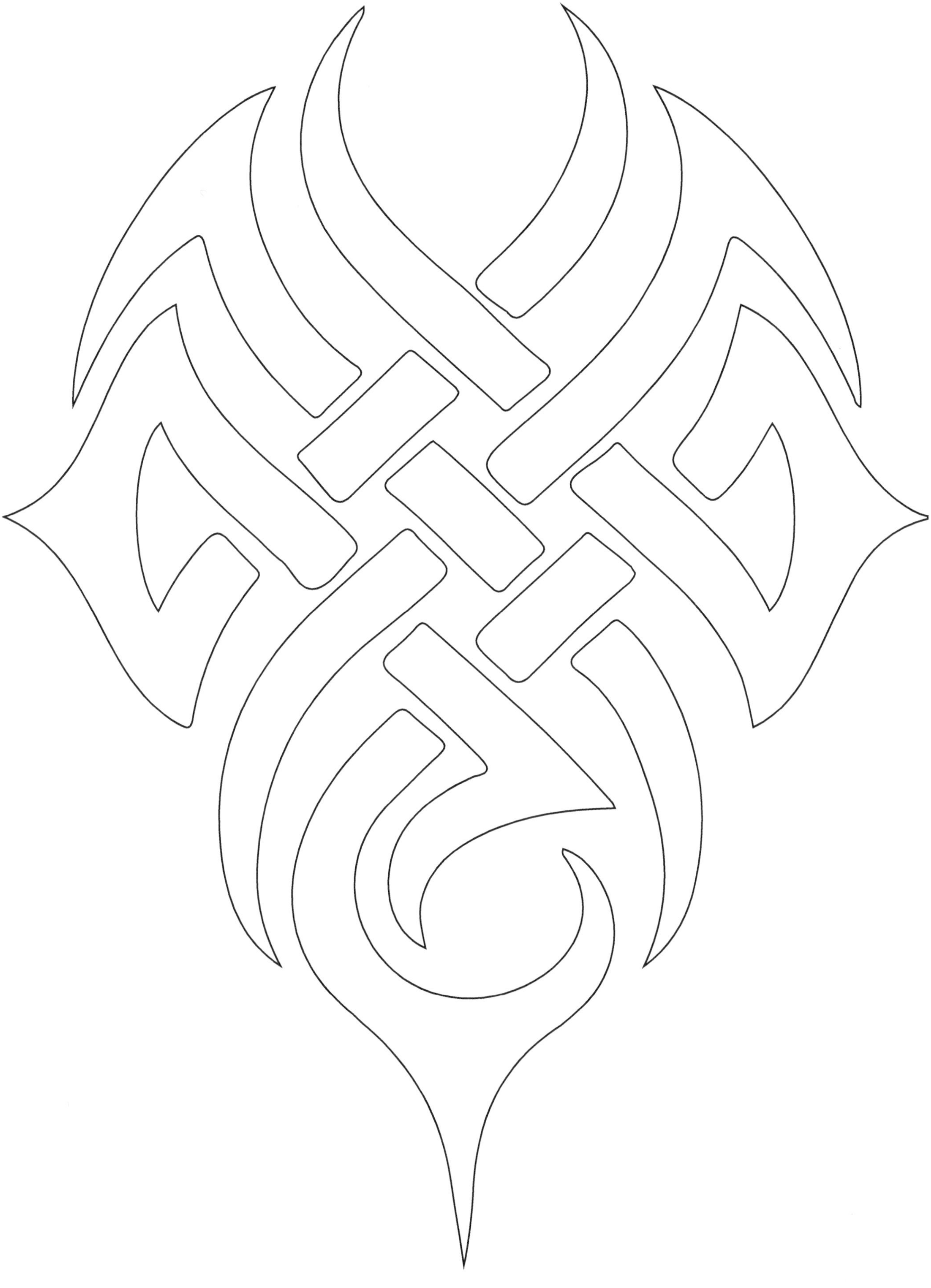

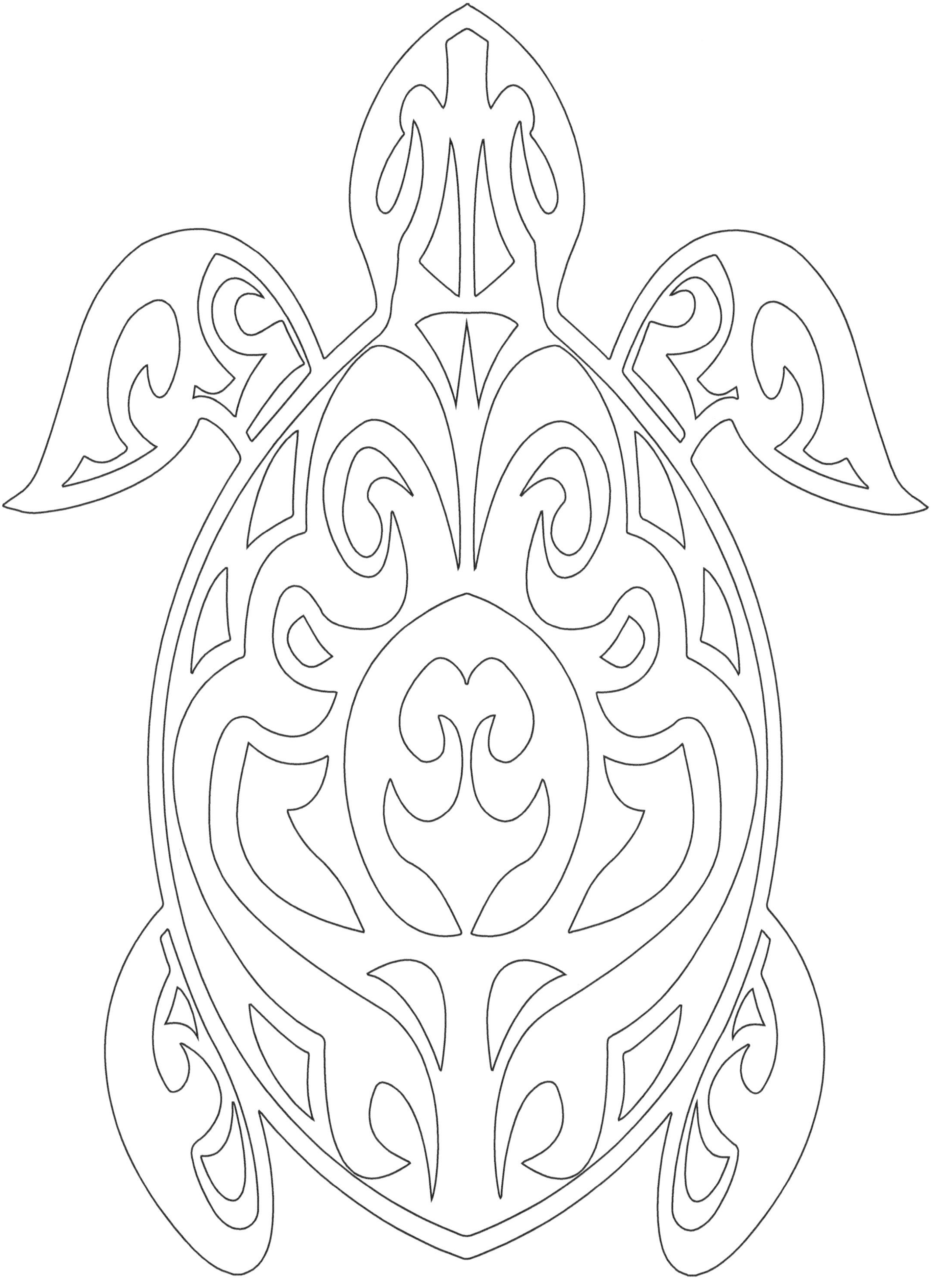

www.ingramcontent.com/pod-product-compliance
Lightning Source LLC
Chambersburg PA
CBHW080641190526
45169CB00009B/3454
* 9 7 8 1 5 3 0 1 0 9 0 7 4 *